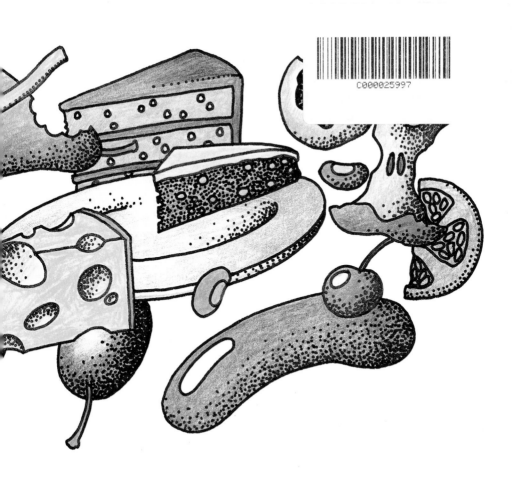

ERFUL THINGS WITH
'S THEM OUT' herb shriner

NEARER MY GOURD TO THEE

anchovy and cleopatra

PIE aaaaaaaaggh (squared)
SIMON DREW'S BOOK ON FOOD AND DRINK

Drawings and Verses
by Simon Drew

salmon
and delilah

ANTIQUE COLLECTORS' CLUB

to
caroline
and to
buzz, tony and carol

ISBN 1 85149 410 3

British Library Cataloguing-in-Publication Data
A catalogue record for this book is available from the British Library

Published and printed in England by the Antique Collectors' Club Ltd., Woodbridge, Suffolk on Consort Royal Satin from Donside Mill, Aberdeen, Scotland

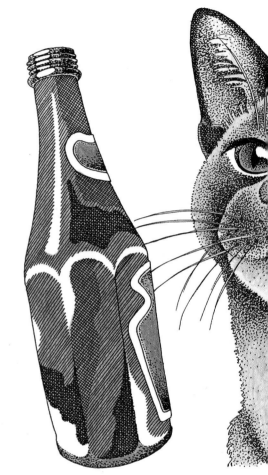

shake, O shake t...
none'll come, an...

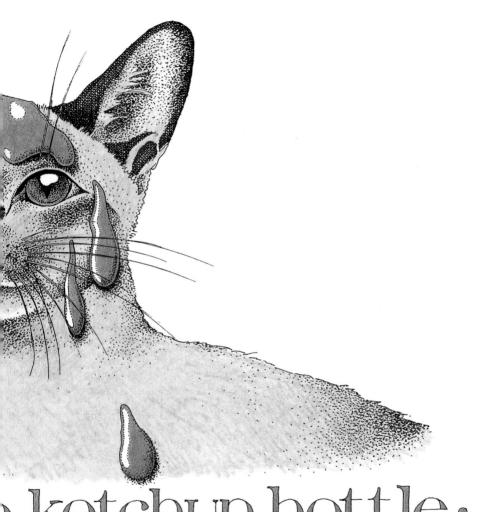

e ketchup bottle;
then a lot'll.
ogden nash

I am not a vegetarian
I'm a vegetarian b

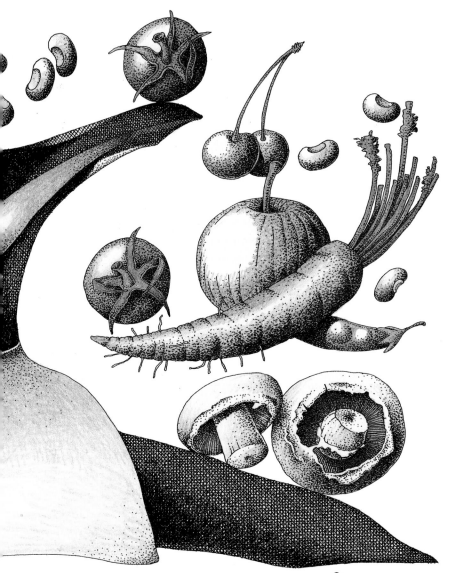

ecause I love animals;
ause I hate plants

a. w. brown

You've never haddock so good

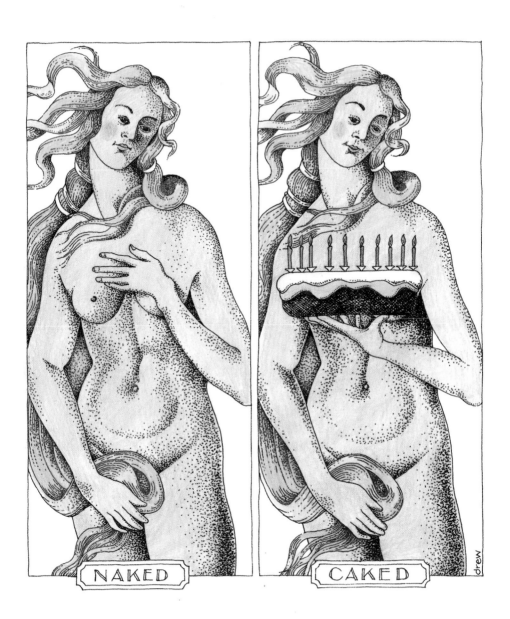

NAKED

CAKED

HAPPY BIRTHDAY

CAT·A·M

ERINGUE

Last Christmas Aunt Flo bought the turkey
but found out the thing wasn't dead
so she gave it a dress and some sequins
and called it a fairy instead.

Rex was very proud
of his coat de bone

How to cross the equator
(whilst eating safely)

Here is advice for the keeping.
You must never spill milk and start weeping
and sow plenty of corn for good reaping;
avoid any toms that are peeping.
Count sheep till you find that you're sleeping
and it's better before you go leaping
     to have looked.

chapter 2.

On the day that you cross the equator
though you travel by liner or freighter
if you want to survive until later
avoid any large alligator
unless you're assured by the waiter
     that it's cooked.

spot the most likely:

cute cat
with flippers

flute cat
with kippers

international cuisine

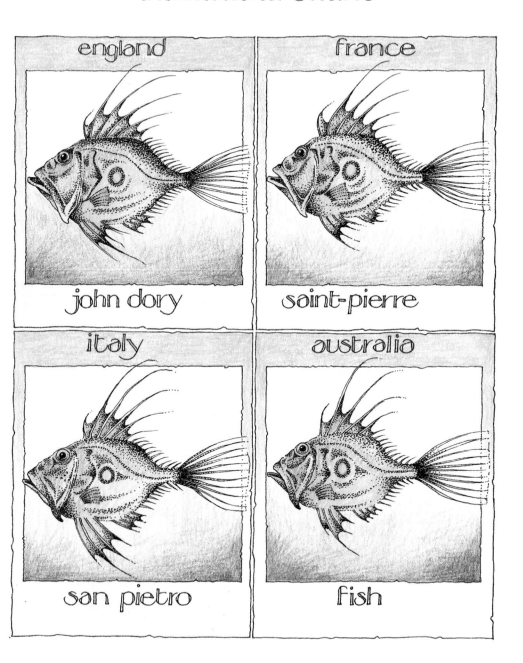

RECIPE

1 egg
2 plums
3 tablespoons of sugar
many peas
       1 comb
       of honey
       taken from the hives
       of Spanish bees
1 ounce
of silver nutmeg
carried here by tradesmen
from
overseas
       1 sprig of
       mistletoe
       picked from near the top
       of apple trees
1 tiny piece
of fluff
from the pocket
       where you keep
your front door keys
       1 cougar's whisker
       blown to you
       on a cool and friendly
       summer breeze

     ..... mix

ADVICE TO A MODERN CHEF

Remember in the sixties
when lettuce was a garnish
and if you wanted shiny cakes
you used a tin of varnish.

o

Presentation now is king:
vegetables mean nothing.
And always talk of 'farci' when
you really mean it's stuffing.

o

Sprinkle pungent dressings
over salad leaves of fashion;
sear the scallops well tonight
in flying pans of passion.

o

Combinations should be strange:
try marmalade with bacon.
If you're asked for steak well done,
the customer's mistaken.

mole marinière

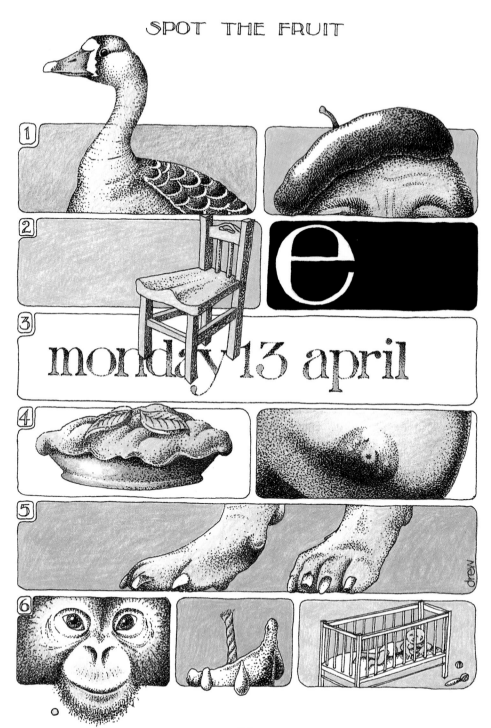

27

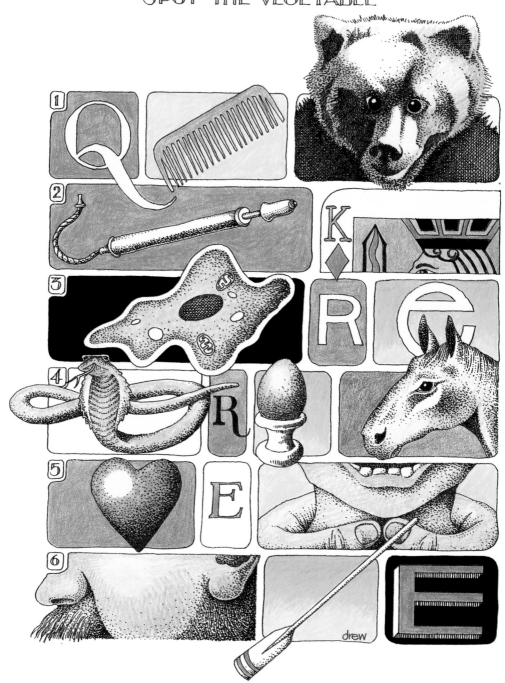

SPOT THE WINE

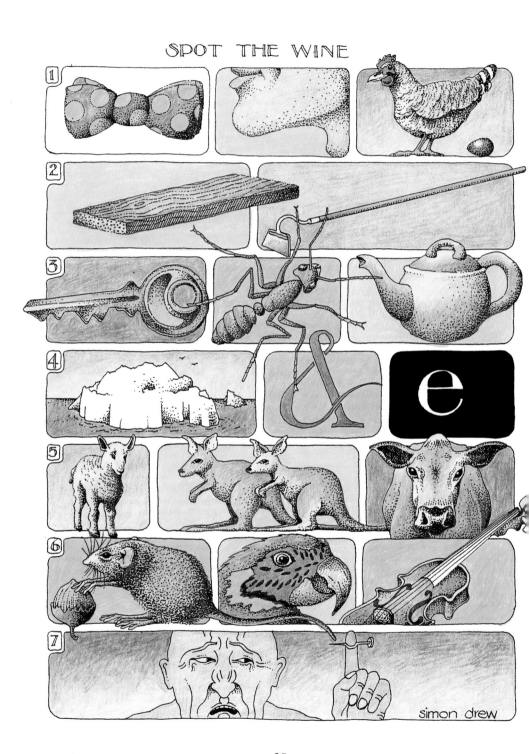

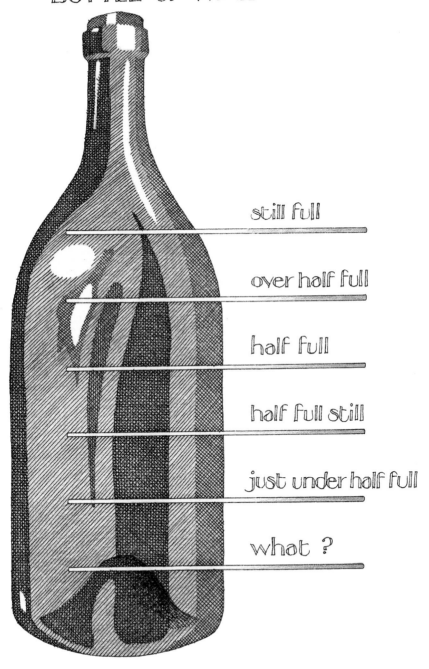

ANALYSIS OF A
BOTTLE OF WINE

still full

over half full

half full

half full still

just under half full

what ?

BEEF EN

OUNTER

THE CASE OF THE MISSING CAKE

JUDGE: Step forward the accused.
You acted out of greed.
Innocent or guilty?
Tell us how you plead.

ACCUSED: I acted out of hunger
Does that make me wrong?
I haven't eaten since the spring:
for me that's far too long.

PROSECUTOR: Did you break and enter?
Was it smash and grab?
Did you go by underground?
Did you take a cab?

DEFENCE: Where were you on Tuesday?
Were you with your wife?
Is it not important
that you've never owned a knife?

ACCUSED: What's a knife, your lordship?
I've always kept the law.
Is it now illegal
to be so sadly poor?

PROSECUTOR: So let us see the weapon
you used to carve the bun.
Weren't you caught red-handed?
We have a smoking gun.

continued
⟶

the
accused

the
prosecutor

the judge

exhibit A

witness:
wing doughnut

the evidence

the case of the missing cake (continued)...

JUDGE: Did he leave a footprint?
          Could we find a way
          to search among his whiskers
          and look for DNA?

POLICEMAN: The little thief was loutish;
          of navy rum he reeked.
          And so we used some force, m'lud
          and after that he squeaked.

PROSECUTOR: And so with this admission
          the case seems fairly clear.
          The evidence has added up:
          it's just as I would fear.

JUDGE: What's the longest sentence
          for felonies like these?
          I think I'm going to jail you
          and throw away the keys.

ACCUSED: Oh yes, I've just remembered:
          whoever did this crime,
          I was at a party
          with your lordship at the time.

JUDGE: Now you come to say so
          it all seems plain to me.
          The law has been miscarried:
          I'll let you off scot free.

the end

witness:
angel cake

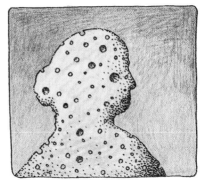

witness:
victoria sponge

witness: sherwood
forest gateau

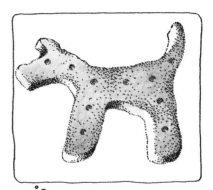

witness:
dog biscuit

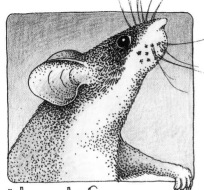

the defence

police witness

the witch guide to baby recipes:

roast kid

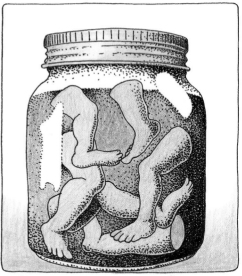

leg mayonnaise

the paté of tiny feet

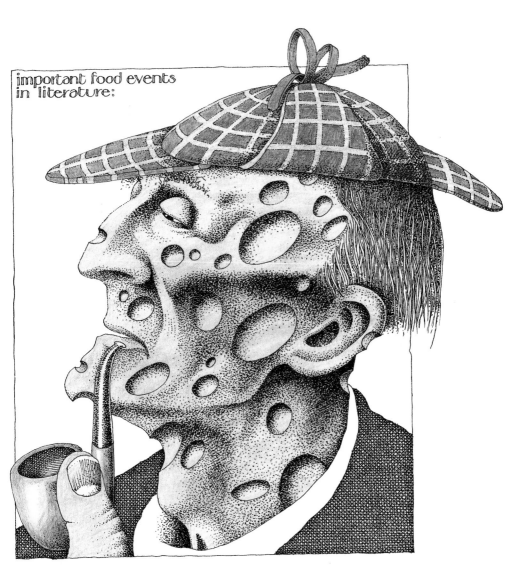

important food events
in literature:

"Emmental, my dear Watson"

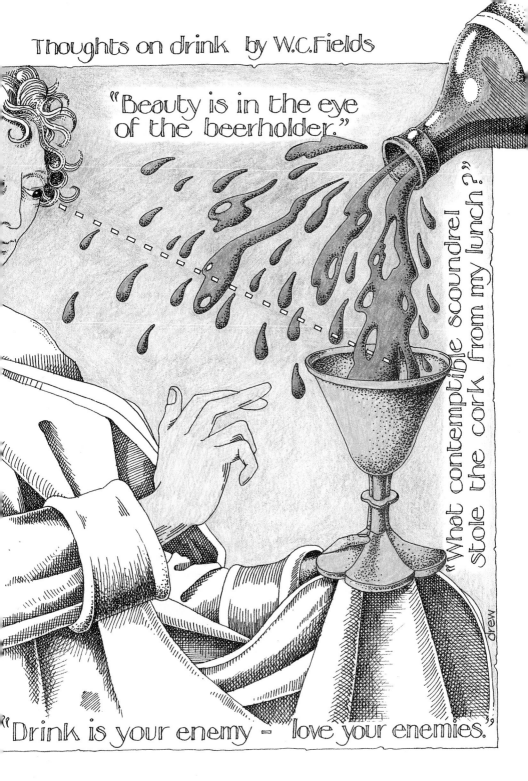

Lunch with Shakespeare

When Shakespeare was writing
                    Richard the Third
it seems that he left out a course
for above all the battle a cry could
                    be heard:
'A horse, I could just eat a horse.'

how to celebrate bass teal day...

Preparing a carp for cooking

Pick out your fish from its watery school:
always select the best scholars.
Then take out the entrails
        (it isn't too cruel)
unless it's a fish full of dollars.

44

the origins of meals on wheels:

cow, boys and engines

RECIPE FOR DISASTER

Crack a fresh egg
            with a half pint of milk
and beat it from dusk until dawn.
Make into omelettes with edges of silk
then add in the shell of a prawn.

With pepper
        and garlic
        and basil
        and bay
        and plentiful helpings of corn:
mix it together the old-fashioned way
with half of a sneeze and a yawn.

Then put in a cupboard
            and wait for a day
and a stork in a teacup is born.

the knight who invented champagne

'NO WOMAN HAS EVER
WHILE HE WAS DOIN